LOVE WITHOUT A STORY

Arundhathi Subramaniam is an award-winning poet and writer on spirituality and culture. Winner of the inaugural Khushwant Singh Memorial Prize for Poetry in 2015, the Raza Award for Poetry and the International Piero Bigongiari Prize, she divides her time between Bombay (the city she loves and loves to hate), an ashram in South India, and New York. She has published three books of poetry in Britain with Bloodaxe, *Where I Live: New & Selected Poems* (2009), which combines selections from her first two Indian collections, *On Cleaning Bookshelves* and *Where I Live*, with new work; *When God Is a Traveller* (2014), a Poetry Book Society Choice which was shortlisted for the T.S. Eliot Prize, won the inaugural Khushwant Singh Prize at the Jaipur Literary Festival, and was awarded the International Piero Bigongiari Prize in Italy; and *Love Without a Story* (2020).

She has also written *The Book of Buddha* (Penguin, 2005) and *Sadhguru: More Than a Life* (Penguin, 2010), co-edited *Confronting Love* (Penguin, 2005), an anthology of Indian love poems in English, and edited *Pilgrim's India: An Anthology* (Penguin, 2011) and *Eating God: A Book of Bhakti Poetry* (2014).

ARUNDHATHI SUBRAMANIAM

Love without a Story

BLOODAXE BOOKS

ISBN: 978 1 78037 516 8

This UK edition first published 2020 by
Bloodaxe Books Ltd,
Eastburn,
South Park,
Hexham,
Northumberland NE46 1BS.

First published in India in 2019 by Context,
an imprint of Westland Publications Private Ltd

www.bloodaxebooks.com
For further information about Bloodaxe titles
please visit our website and join our mailing list
or write to the above address for a catalogue

Supported using public funding by
ARTS COUNCIL
ENGLAND

Cover design: Neil Astley & Pamela Robertson-Pearce.

Printed in Great Britain by Bell & Bain Limited, Glasgow, Scotland, on
acid-free paper sourced from mills with FSC chain of custody certification.

CONTENTS

I Grew Up in an Age of Poets

Best to meet in poems

EUNICE DE SOUZA

I grew up in an age of poets
who told me joy

was for cabbages
until I found

that beneath their smoking
empires of sulphur

there lay a shiver
of doubt,

that they wondered,
as I did,

about what it might mean
to be leafy,

to wilt,
to be damaged sometimes

by upstart caterpillars
and still stay green –

chaotically, wetly, powerfully
green.

Now I meet poets
who exchange visiting cards,

who are best friends with the dentist,
all dankness deodorised,

their poems cool seashells,
their laughter splintered eggshells,

poets who never seem
to wonder

about cabbages
at all.

Still best to meet in poems.

Deleting the Picture

(for AA, 1967-2015)

It's 2005
and we are almost glamorous,
the five of us –

the chairs are cane,
my shirt batik,
the sunshine Goa
              and Heineken.

We're past the clumsy brutality
of eighteen –

we've deleted
makeshift faces,
borrowed persuasions,
stances without journeys.

We've forgiven the treacheries
of student seminars,
wrong addresses
at different ends of the city,
digressions of faith.

No edge
to our voices anymore
when we say Zen
          or Gramsci.

We're wearing
the dumb happy
of holiday
and wearing it well –

              and there's always so much sun.

Against limewashed churches
and cashew plantations of melted green
we're laughing hard,
beer-glazed, sand-drizzled, stoned
on Sgt Pepper and Kishore Kumar.

And there's the other picture, look,
where arms entwined,
we're bathed in fierce siesta light
and seem to know this moment
                    is teetering
on the verge
of never again.

It isn't difficult, of course,
to skip the nostalgia,

to fast forward
the embarrassment
of memory,

to speak,
as others do,
of calcium
rather than satori.

So, the morning I heard
it wasn't difficult to turn efficient,

to delete
pictures of humming birds
and cardamom tea

and the air ticket you emailed me,
never knowing it would be
the one to your funeral.

It gets easier, friend,
with age,
to delete, plan breakfast,
turn the page.

It would have been easier still
if you hadn't deleted the sun.

A Theory of Wandering

I remember the day I lay in bed
with a fever

that vanished as soon as the school bus
turned the corner, after which I spent

hours composing a tune
for a poem on Orpheus to sing

on my sister's return.
It was a rainy day in Bombay, so easy

to splice into the cypress groves
and briny Aegean breezes

of a classical spring
alive with lutesong

(as the forests of Vrindavan
once probably quickened in wonder

to maddening flutesong)
and given a chance today, I'd be ready

to hijack a school bus
and set sail full steam ahead

to Mystras or to Crete
and once there, to waft

back again on foaming lute waves
into a sleepy Bombay apartment

with its peepul tree and breezes from Oman
always ready to build

vehicles of truancy –
    ships, lutes, flutes, songs –

ready to be waterborne, airborne, etherborne,
    and on every attendance roster,

always
    a little more absent

than present.

And Where It Might End

It's not the mind.
It's the body
that grows parochial,

that hungers,
turns peevish,

recognises
its own alluvium,

following a hunch
less cultural than perhaps
            botanical –

a soil sense –

the need for this slurry of grass, warmed
by the dreamless slumber

of this particular earthworm,
more compost still than organism,

the great churn,
hypnotic,
amniotic,

of dust, mulch, silence,
    seasoned with woodsmoke,

    a peasant's voice charred
with tobacco, fermented film song,

shot through
    by a tremor
    of tropical sun.

And so, the awakening happens,
    gradual

    and then in its own way,
                    startling –

ready and serenely
biodegradable,

the body wants to be nowhere
but here.

Mitti

As a child
I ate mud.

It tasted of grit and peat
and wild churning

and something I could never find
a name for.

Later I became
a moongazer

always squinting through
windows,

believing freedom
was aerial

until I figured that the moon
was a likely mud-gazer

longing for the thick sludge
of gravity,

the promiscuous thrill
of touch,

the licence to make,
break, remake,

and so I uncovered
the old role of poets –

to be messengers
between moon and mud –

and began to learn the many
languages of earth

that have nothing to do with nations
and atlases

and everything to do
with the ways

of earwigs,
the pilgrim trail of roots

and the great longing of life to hold
and be held,

and the irrepressible human love
of naming:

ooze, mire, manure, humus, dirt, silt
mould, loam, soil, slush, clay, shit,
mannu, matope, barro,
tin, ni, luto, fango...

All have their place, I found,
in the democracy of tongues,

none superior,
none untranslatable,

all reminders
of the anthem

of muck
of which we are made,

except when June clouds capsize
over an Arabian Sea

and a sleeping city
awakens to an ache so singular

that for just a moment,
it could have no name

other than that
where sound meets scent

and a slurry of matter
meets a slick lunatic wetness:

mitti.

Just that. Nothing else will do.

Finding Dad

When parents die,
you hunt for clues
in strips of Sorbitrate,
immaculate handwriting,
unopened cologne
and in evening air,
traces of baritone.

You believe
they must add up
to a story larger
than the one you knew,

larger than the face that looked up
abstractedly
from a book –
sovereign, mysterious –
while a cricket commentary crackled inanely
on a television screen,

until you discover
the old fallacy –
the dots never joined,
the clues never worked,

that even when they were around
parents were always
piecemeal,

themselves just a clue

and the only way
to their centre
is the secret way
past the epidermis of things –

the carnival path of self-
forgetfulness. Always has been.

And so, when fathers
disperse
into fire and ocean
and sputtering sky,
into ferris-wheeling limb
and splintering desire,

there is no following
except through dance,

the great charring dance
in which they stand revealed –

divested, fallible,
    whole –

whole
in the body's gentle democracy,
whole
in the heart's stubborn partisanship
you knew as love.

        Your Dad's crazy love.

The strange thing about love

is that it melts you

into an amateur,

never again a professional
            even
            on the subject of yourself.

*

The strange thing about love

is that you disagree,

disagree wildly,

and then figure it's wiser

to dance.

*

The strange thing about love

is that it evicts you
from the land of echoes
you thought was home

and leads you to
friends

sitting
under the stars

in ancient
bewilderment.

La Verna

It was a day riddled with signs
for each of us –

Italian agnostic,
American Unitarian Buddhist,
Hindu seeker.

We went because our friend –
gay, Catholic, Tuscan –
recommended it. 'Jesus is God
and God is One,' he said,
'and that should leave out San Francesco,
but I love him still,
and I love him even more
when I go to La Verna.'

And so, we went
one afternoon in March,

plunged into a delirium
of boulder, rain and spinning
sky, suspended between the Tiber
and the Arno, between wild geology
and keeling light, where the wind
is falcon flight and gravity aerial,

where the sombre white owl
has seen it all –
      rock melting into forest,
      wolf into lamb,
      sky into mineral,
      gnarled root into cosmos,

where faith is a gaunt wooden crucifix
against an ache of valley,

and prayer
the cry of kestrels entangled
in ancient beechwood
and the spillage of light
through wind-shirred cloud.

And there was the bright-eyed Russian
we met outside the chapel
of St Mary of the Angels
who told me her spiritual guide
was Indian

       and we grew silent
to find we carried in our bags
the picture of the same fakir
with quizzical gaze and dirty robe.

It felt like there was something that day
for each of us.

It could have been
the gasp of precipice scarred
     by ravine.

It could have been
that gentle saint of the valley scarred
     by love.

We never knew
and were none the wiser afterwards

about whether there was one
or many

     or none at all.

But high above the valley of Casentino
there was a day in March –

we'd agree,
the three of us –

that couldn't be tamed
by arithmetic.

A First Monsoon Again

(Bombay, July 2016)

At first
it's nostalgia –

a downpour of kisses
under a weeping umbrella,

a euphoria
of gulmohur,

an eternity
of adrak chai,

every moment
the memory of a previous one

when the skies were crazier,
love purer,
life simpler,

when the heart was Malabar,
the spirit Arabian,

desire Coromandel,
laughter more Gene Kelly

and words like baarish
and mazhai

were headier,
truer.

The first rains
are always
this plagiarism of yearning,

every moment
an echo of another –

the thunder the roar
of an outlawed god

whose hair is a foaming green river
through which seahorse

and carp dart drunkenly
around a crescent moon,

and every dark cloud a courier
from a classical past,

and longing
a rising fever of loam

and thirst for a man whose voice
is blue ash and oatmeal. And wetness.

It takes a long time
to arrive
at this Tuesday-at-elevenness
when we open our windows
to the outrage,
the impossible nowness,
the gasp,
the sock in the chest,
the raving psychosis,
the brazen never-beforeness

and say the word,

our voices alight
with unguarded wonder

and a kind
of pristine terror:

'Monsoon.'

How to Read Indian Myth

(for AS who wonders)

How to read Indian myth?
The way I read Greek, I suppose –

not worrying too much about
foreign names
and plots,

knowing there is never
a single point
to any story,

taking the red hibiscus route
into the skin,

alert to trapdoors, willing
    to blunder a little in the dark,

        slightly drunk
            on Deccan sun,

but with a spring in the step
that knows

we are fundamentally
corky,

built to float,
built to understand,

and the chemical into which we are tumbling
will sustain,
has sustained before,

knows a way through,
knows a way beyond,

knows
the two

aren't separate.

Read it like you would read a love story.
Your own.

Remembering

Friend, when will I have it
both ways,
be with Him
yet not with Him...?

AKKA MAHADEVI
(translated from the Kannada
by A.K. Ramanujan)

Here's what I'm good at.

When you're around,
marinating.

When you're not,
remembering.

Nostalgia is reflex, a spasm
of cortical muscle.

But this remembering isn't habit
or even sentiment.

This remembering
is a slumbering,

allowing main text to drift
into marginalia,
weekday into holiday,

inhaling you
as rumour,
as legend,

and suddenly, as thing,

superbly
    empirical,

with your very own
    local scent
of infinity.

Let me follow river currents
warm with sun,
the ambling storylines
of green lotus stems
and wooden boats.

Let me be that tangle of moonbeam
and plankton

on a journey too pointless
to be pilgrimage,

floating, jamming,
    just jetsamming.

Remembering isn't an art,
more an instinct,

a knowing that there is

nothing limited
about body,

nothing piecemeal
about detail,

nothing at all
    secondhand

about remembering.

Bring on the Screen Savers

And it must be
because I am not ready yet

for this newspaper to mean as much
as a sparrow's nest,

for greeting card verse to mean as much
as Basho,

for some swirling emulsion of infinity
to mean as much

    as you.

And it must be because some words
are juicier still
than others
(incarnadine, emollient, pneuma, love)

and some moments
still more precious.

Let's put a lid on it,
draw the veil,
bring on the screen savers.

Let things not lose their edge,
me not become you.

Let's stop the surfeit
of equality,

cling to a mere a smattering
of hierarchy.

Who wants the big picture?

More light, more colour, more sharpness, more edge.
More you.

More.

   More.

Just more will do.

The Fine Art of Ageing

I

It's not that Avvaiyar
doesn't admire the green impertinence
of sapling bodies

or the way a middle-aged woman
can smile
at an ex-lover, an ex-rival,
and effortlessly attain a kind
of goddesshood.

She's not against play-acting either.
She enjoys the smell of fiction,
knows it's fun to pretend
at immortality.

She knows centuries are separated
by historians, not poets,

that now and then
are divided by
the thinnest membranes
of belief,

that there's not much difference
really

between lush shola grasslands
stunned by a blue fusillade
of kurinji flowers

Avvaiyar: legendary poet and wise woman of Tamil literature. The name
(literally 'respectable old woman') was probably accorded to more than one
poet in the canon.

and urban jungles
moistly evergreen
with people on the make.

But she knows the journey
from goddess to gran,
sylph to hag,
prom queen to queen mum
is longer than most,
more tortuous.

She knows also
folklore has its stories,
newspapers too,
of old kings
dewrinkling
into young men

(a man called Yayati, for instance,
conqueror of free radicals, victor of fine lines,
high on a son's sacrifice, women, fine wines,

collagen, spirulina, vitamin E,
macadamia nuts, extracts of green tea,

triclosan, selenium, propylene glycol,
alpha hydroxy acids, bergamot, retinol).

Avvaiyar makes
another choice.

Spare me the desperation of the old,
she says,
and the puerility of the young.

Spare me the glamour
of being youthful wife to five princes –
Draupadi, the fruit everyone wants to peel.

And spare me the sainthood
of mad women mystics
who peel off their own rind
before others can get to them
    (vaporising
    into the white jasmine scent
    of hagiography).

Avvaiyar makes
another choice –

fearless friend to gods,
ally of peasants,

counsellor to kings,
traveller of the darkest streets,

she walks the world alone.

And on such a path, she says,
it's best to be
a crone.

II

And oh, the relief of being spared
the forest of wet eyes,

the danger years of stickiness
no one warns you about –

quivering stamens,
wild pollination,
moonlight and Persian tuberoses,
the years when everything turns to sap.

Avvaiyar's done with ooze and cream,
Avvaiyar's done with the soggy dream
of being kissed awake by love.

She's done with the nightmare
of smiling and finding she's forgotten
to wear her dentures.

She's so light
she can finally
take herself
seriously.

One way to outwit death, she says,
is to invite it over.

Wear it.

III

Avvaiyar lives in a face
where the civil war
is almost over,

frayed flags of peace hoisted,
cavalry slumbering,
garrison emptied.

Nothing to declare any more, she says,
not even nostalgia

(perhaps just a few ruined keepsakes –
a bottle of limoncello
from a sun-slathered June in Amalfi,
a butterscotch moon from a Tel Aviv hotel,.
a picture of a cat,
        pink-pawed, yogic).

For lovers flatten
into photographs,

photographs
into reminiscence,

reminiscence
into quiet.

And then what's left?

Perhaps just the oldest thing in the world –
love without a story.

IV

Avvaiyar knows that tyrannical
algebra teachers die,

and timid cleaning ladies
with floral aprons too.

She knows oligarchic poets blur
into fussy grandpas,

dashing bankers get dementia
and the prettiest girls in class

slash their wrists in beach homes,
felled by boredom and barbiturates.

She knows the ageing ustad
is eventually ousted

by triglycerides and court politics
(and the silent acolyte
with smouldering eyes and humid palms).

She knows every court must have
its oily pundit,

its bleating groupies,
its sullen cavillers, its jester stoned
on his own demagoguery.

She knows every sangha has its Devadutta
plotting his coup

in a blue swirl of powerlust. She knows
that everyone everywhere

believes they've been wronged,
that history was written by someone else

and that they're always
right.

V

It's then that a boy god enters the picture

and turns it
(as he often does)
into a story
about a fruit.

'So, what's it going to be, Gran,
a hot fruit
or a lukewarm one?'

asks the little boy on the tree,
left cheek bulging with jamun
and laughter.

(Pure cheek really.)

Avvaiyar sighs,
knows the tiresome games
of the young –
trick questions, riddles,
puns, crosswords, wisecracks,
bon mots, limericks, anagrams,

knows little boys grow into
men that scintillate,
men that pontificate,

men that dribble curses,
men that cannot apologise,

grey-faced men,
men that turn love to ash,

men with shiny weapons
and kettledrum agitations,

men with epic stories, epic vanities,
epic bibliographies,
epic epic,

men that make young girls giggle
(and silently plot vengeance),

Vedantin men,
men with restless gazes,

men that sip white wine
and drip Mallarmé.

Avvaiyar sighs.

The thing about age
is seeing through the game
but being able to smile
at those who play it.

'All right,' she says,
'all right, boy,
make it lukewarm.'

VI

And that makes the boy chuckle
and shake a branch

so a fruit rolls
  voluptuously
down a simmering gravel road

  and as Avvaiyar reaches out,
blows off the dust

and is about to sink toothless gums
into purple skin,

the voice asks –

'What's with the huffing, Gran?
      Fruit too hot for you?'

The jamun stays uneaten
and as a hillside swelters
in fierce noonlight,

a cloud appears
out of nowhere
and Avvaiyar shivers,

knows enough about atmospherics
to figure

there's more at work here
than a smart aleck
with dreams of world domination.

She looks up
eyes squinting,
wrinkles fading

joints uncreaking
crowsfeet unravelling,

as before her eyes
a jamun-cheeked boy
detonates

in a thunderclap
of turquoise and tourmaline

into the god that rides the peacock
whose tail is an audacity

of eyes, infinite and unblinking
against a raging sky.

VII

I don't think Avvaiyar turned young again.
She didn't need to.

But she threw off her last disguise –
wise woman,
keeper of the faith,

and settled down to being
what she'd always been –

a traveller with an appetite
for conversation,
a boy god's best friend,

composer of one-line poems –
epics whitened
by a blizzard of silence –

and learned to forgive
men with puzzled eyes

who invite you to share nothing more
against life's Bokhara winters

than the campfire
of the heart.

And she finds another way
to walk the razor's edge,

between lush shola grasslands
stunned by a blue fusillade
of kurinji flowers

and urban jungles
moistly evergreen
with people on the make,

learning to trust only the wisdom
that sings,

learning the equipoise
of crumble,

not looking
for a point,

knowing the point, if any,
is a shared fruit and laughter,

knowing there's no sadly
or happily ever after,

and finds a new credo for mendicants
a new paradigm:

stay molten-tongued (never lukewarm)
even if ragged in rhyme,

unhurried, forever out of step,
always on time.

Missing Friends

In another land
my friends are sad.

The planet is smouldering, they say,
like never before.

I remember the times we ordered
our brun maskas,
ran fingers over formica tables sticky
with kolatkar, pound, almodovar,
clarice lispector,
nammalvar.

At times we'd disagree:

teilhard de chardin, he'd say,
salim chishti,

tukaram, you'd reply, pinkola estés,
(or irrelevantly, agatha christie)

and we'd shake our heads sadly –
gandhigandhigandhi.

It was a world of common nouns
we inhabited –
comforting really

(not unlike that darker
age of innocence
when I thought Coca Cola
was spelt lower case
and came from a fruit).

We'd laugh immoderately
over the haiku poet
whose cv was never
a haiku,

spend the ritual half hour
on god, on death.

In another land
my friends are sad,

their tables still sticky
with octavio paz and simmering teas.

The right and left have failed us, they say,
then head to eat lebanese.

Some days
I miss friends.

Parents

They vanish as abruptly
as they appear,

busy perfecting
the art of truancy
when they send you away to school.

They cry 'wolf' many times over
but when you turn for a moment,
they melt away,
velvet-pawed, sure-footed,
into the night.

Parents II

They litter
    your cells with memory,
    your head with echoes,

never quite prepare you
    for tradesmen at three,
    share certificates,

reminding you that the big truths
    are never oracular,

just slippers outside a bathroom,

and in cupboards,
the routine ambush –

preverbal, intimate,
blindly illiterate –

of genes.

When Landscape Becomes Woman

I was eight when I looked
through a keyhole

and saw my mother in the drawing room
in her hibiscus silk sari,

her fingers slender
around a glass of iced cola

and I grew suddenly shy
for never having seen her before.

I knew her well, of course –
serene undulation of blue mulmul,
wrist serrated by thin gold bangle,
gentle convexity of mole
on upper right arm,
and her high arched feet –
better than I knew myself.

And I knew her voice
like running water –
            ice cubes in cola.

But through the keyhole
at the grown-up party
she was no longer
geography.

She seemed to know
how to incline her neck,
just when to sip
her swirly drink
and she understood the language
of baritone voices and lacquered nails
and words like Emergency.

I could have watched her all night.

And that's how I discovered
that keyholes always reveal more
than doorways.

That a chink in a wall
is all you need
to tumble
into a parallel universe.

That mothers are women.

This Could Be Enough

We are warm with Mojitos
and your stories of Poland

and your verities about men
who fear intimacy.

This sisterhood could almost be enough
and still it isn't, we know.

And those men –
the ones that fear intimacy

    and the ones that don't –
they won't be enough either.

But this evening
of muddled longing and rage,

your laughter acacia
and honey,

me in my red skirt,
you in your linen smock,

the man at the far table
glowering in lust,

the ditsy waiter
(his gaze greened by a memory
of rain holidays in Mangalore),

the embrace
of this gently hysterical city,

and the hours deemed happy
by the gods
of Tuesday night,

is all we really need to remember.

Ten years later,
    and maybe sooner,

we won't ask for more.

Tongue

The tongue is alone and tethered in its mouth

JOHN BERGER

The man in front of me
is reading
a balance sheet.

He is smiling, his gaze
shimmying between columns,
effortlessly
bilingual.

And though a little drunk
on the liquor of profit

I like to think he is not immune
to the sharp beauty

of integers, simmering
with their own inner life,

and I wonder if he feels
the way I do sometimes
    around words,

waiting for them to lead me
past the shudder
    of tap root
        past the inkiness
            of groundwater
                to those places

where all tongues meet –

    calculus, Persian, Kokborok, flamenco,

the tongue sparrows know, and accountants,
and those palm trees at the far end
of holiday photographs,

    your tongue,
    mine,

the kiss that knows
from where the first songs sprang,

    forested and densely plural,

the kiss that knows
no separation.

Let Me Be Adjective

And so, the verb is all.

But I'm not ready for it yet.

I tie knots
every now and then

to dam the flow,
to pretend

I am thing,
I am thing

and to pretend
you are too,

more thing than I,
worthier of being described.

And until the knots come undone
as one day they must,

let me modify,
qualify,
anoint,
counterpoint,
apostrophise,
parenthesise,
invent,
dissent.
Let me take wing.
Let me sing

you.

I suppose I'm asking,
like the old bards did,
to be your garland,

not always tenderly floral,

just a little tart,
a little contrary,

the kind that isn't always allowed
within walled gardens.

But even as I meander,
              let my trail
                    be the thread
      that completes the circle
I long to make around you.

Love, let me be adjective.

Let There Be Grid

If my gaze must expand
to match

the altitude
of my desire,

the arc of my arms
widen

to include more than
it leaves out,

let me never lose the moment
that startled

this poem into being.

Let it April me over
to the great salted wilderness
of harbour

that is you,

    your eyes a festival
    of laughter,
    the scent of your skin
       vetiver,
           champaka,
your mouth
ocean-dark, gentler than dream.

Let the windows stay closed.

Until the world is neighbourhood,
until emptiness has biography,

until you
are on the other side,

let there be grid.

The Need for Nests

This is the moment
when it returns –

    the need to build nests,

when it isn't enough to follow
the trails

of cranes that leap
    in a silver flash of tailwind

from coastal palm trees
        straight
    to the moon,

when the only thing that will settle me
is your arms, the long night

and the friendly dialogue
of slumbering breath,

lamplight, animality,
the cave

and the promise of laughter
in the morning.

Who knows, perhaps I'll even get there,
but let it not be alone.

Let it not be alone.

With you
    the flight is pure song
    and the grand tempest
        of argument.

With you
the wings of cranes
are warmed by the heat
of local fish markets.

With you
even the moon smells
                    of mackerel.

Ninda-stuti

Complaint
is only possible
while living in the suburbs
of God

HAFIZ
(translated from the Persian
by Daniel Ladinsky)

We are not impressed
by your platoons of admirers,
your raging eyes,
your guest lists,
your visiting cards,
your seven-horse chariots,
your LED screens.

We aren't minor either.

If it's about choosing
between big and small,
form and vacancy,
we choose neither.

If you're playing the game,
we are too.

We come from a tribe
that knows that a versified tantrum
is a kind of prayer.

We turn invective
into love

Ninda-stuti: The genre of Indian sacred literature (*ninda:* abuse or blame; *stuti:* song of praise) that considers anger or irony a valid form of devotion.

(salty, sometimes
sulphuric)

and love
into obscenity.

Our longing reaches for the stars.

Domesticated
    by our fury,
even the skies turn
        terrestrial.

And the rest of the time
the Earth

        – this lunatic suburb –

is plenty.

Song for Catabolic Women

We're bound for the ocean
and a largesse of sky,
we're not looking for the truth
or living a lie.

We're coming apart,
we're going downhill,
the fury's almost done,
we've had our fill.

We're passionate, ironic
angelic, demonic,
clairvoyant, rational
wildly Indian, anti-national.

We're not trying to make our peace
not itching for a fight,
we don't need your shade
and we don't need your light.

We know charisma isn't contagious
and most rules are egregious.

We're catabolic women.

We've known the refuge of human arms,
the comfort of bathroom floors,
we've stormed out of rooms,
thrown open the doors.

We've figured the tricks to turn rage
into celebration,
we know why the oldest god dances
at every cremation.

We've kissed in the rose garden,
been the belles of the ball,
hidden under bedcovers
and we've stood tall.

We're not interested in camouflage
or self-revelation,
not looking for a bargain
or an invitation.

We're capable of stillness
even as we gallivant,
capable of wisdom
even as we rant.

Look into our eyes,
you'll see we're almost through.
We can be kind but we're not really
thinking of you.

We don't remember names
and we don't do Sudoku.
We're losing EQ and IQ,
forgetting to say please and thank you.

We're catabolic women

We've never ticked the right boxes,
never filled out the form,
our dharma is tepid,
our politics lukewarm.

We've had enough of earnestness
and indignation
but still keep the faith
in conversation.

We're wily Easterners enough
to argue nirvana and bhakti,
talk yin and yang,
Shiva and Shakti.

When we're denied a visa
we fall back on astral travel
and when samsara gets intense
we simply unravel.

We're unbuilding now,
unperpetuating,
unfortifying,
disintegrating.

We're caterwauling,
        catastrophic,
        shambolic,
        cataclysmic,
        catabolic women.

The End of the World

The end of the world, you say,
is the escalator going backwards,

bird withdrawing
into leaf,

tortoise freezing
into rock,

the syncopated sniffles
of Indian television's daughters

dissolving
into a pink sea of Revlon.

And at fifty, I know
the need for warmth

begins in the knees,
and sometimes ends there.

The story of longing
and union

is overheated.
Irrelevant really.

The end of the world?
Just you and I withdrawing, love,

from this conversation.

Shorthand

The body speaks shorthand,
coded,
yet blazingly simple.

To hold each other all night
is all we want

and still
we sit apart,
tell stories,

not trusting
the only art
that matters right now –

stenography.

The Monk

(who's been in silence
sixteen years)

writes me a note
at a yak tea stall

skirted by ragged prayer flags
in a grey hiccupping wind

on the road to Kailash.
His face is scarp and fissure

and gleaming teeth.
He spends each day

cleaning his shrine.
'It's worth it,' he laughs.

'I clean the shrine,
it cleans me.'

He was a spare parts dealer
in a time he barely remembers

before he was tripped up
by something that felt
like a granite mountain in reverse,

the deepest pothole
he's ever known,

too deep
to be called love,

that turned him into a spare part himself,

utterly dispensable,
wildly unemployed.

'And if there is another lifetime
this is what I'd ask for,' he says

(and now he doesn't laugh):

'Same silence. Same cleaning.'

The Lover

The woman doesn't call herself
a saint,

just a lover
of a saint

who's been dead four hundred years.

She doesn't see people
on weekdays

but her master tells her
we're safe,

so she calls us in to where she sits,
her body blazing
in its nakedness,
     a crumpled afterthought,

its tummyfold and breastsag
and wild spiraling nipple
reminding us that life
is circles –
crazy, looping, involuting, dazzling
circles.

She tells us
the world calls her a whore.

She told her master about it too
but he only said,

'The rest of the world serves
many masters –
family, money, lovers, bosses,

fame, power, money, money,
in endless carousels –

       the crazy autopilot
       of samsara.

But you, love, think only of me.
Who's the whore here?'

Outside the window
the sun is a red silk lampshade

over a great soiled bedspread,
ricocheting in the wind.

The Bus to Ajmer

We're a circus troupe of a kind,

sixteen Pakistanis, one Indian,
juddering away
on a bus to Ajmer –

twelve men, eyes kohl-rimmed,
one beside me, his body rigid

with conviction, gaze itinerant
with desire, eyeing

the breathless woman from Islamabad
whose conversation is unstoppered, damp

with a sadness she isn't aware of,
in front of whom bobs and fumes

a self-proclaimed fakir,
all costume and comic despair,

waving wild hands at
Sunny bhaiyya, stolid tour leader,

father of four, our circus ringmaster,
accountant from Lahore.

And sitting by the driver,
the Karachi poet,

his speech softened
by Charminar cigarettes

and all the old confusions,
        achingly familiar.

Politesse is abundant.
I welcome them to my Indian saint,
they welcome me to their faith.

At the shrine the twelve men unwind
into malangs,

whirling slowly
into a place
of studied ecstasy

that is suddenly,
        jaggedly,
a kind of abandon.

The fakir sings,
the poet fidgets,
Sunny bhaiyya prays.

There is some envy in our gaze.
Excluded briefly
from the euphoria,
the sad woman and I
close our eyes.

We are a circus still
at the end of it

but cooled by marble,
heated by song,

quieted by the tale
of yet another madman

caught up in a sandstorm of love
lurching down to Hind
from distant Persia
in a blunder of fever and instinct
that some call mission,

our disguises are just a bit
askew,

bodies more provisional,
stories less italicised,

breath more rationed,
certainties more unlaced

(as the old Khwaja,
crazy vagrant from Sistan,
might have wanted).

The poet and I exchange addresses.

In Short

All the time
that you believed
you were housed,
you were actually outside,

nose pressed flat
against the panes
of brightly lit windows

and you forgot that people
are also panes
you press your nose against,
leaving behind a steamblot,

that you can never climb in
for good,
however hard you try.

And one day you realise
you're a pane too, freckled
by your own rigmaroles of vapour

and all your life you've done nothing
but make hectic designs
on the glass.

And you're still
outside.

The Problem with Windows

The problem with windows
isn't through a glass darkly.

The problem is
through a glass stickily.

But now when you look through windows
with a gaze that for just a little while
isn't flypaper,

your breath
tumble-dried,
spin-cycled,
dehumidified,
crinkled,

every moment
at an airport coffee shop

could be
(and sometimes even is)

an indifferent café frappé,
no more, no less,

and it's funny too, knowing
that the man with the brown briefcase

looking in idly
on the other side

wants fleetingly,
unreasonably
(and has no clue why),

to be you.

Been There

With every step ahead
I've always left something behind.

Earlier,
again and again,
        the heart,
storm-tossed,
wetter than the Konkan coast in July.

It's easier now,
the heart's more my own,
the windscreen less blurry,

But some part of the self
still trails behind –

a disconsolate schoolboy
kicking a stone
along an evening road,

not shipwrecked
by pain or fury,

just accustomed
to being told

he must be patient,
he must wait,

accustomed
to being told that one day,

but not for a long time yet,

he'll be grown up,
he'll understand.

Backbencher

The backbencher
has long legs,

imperturbable face,
ink blot on uniform,

a smile sometimes described
as saturnine,

knows
there's a window behind her

and the raw mangoes outside
are just an arm span away.

The backbencher knows
how to be last on rosters,

how to saunter
unhurriedly

to her seat every morning,
knows that when her name

is called, finally,
it is because

what she wants to know
is now seething with impatience,

lonely,
bloody

lonely,
and longing,

longing desperately to be known.

If It Must Be Now

When glaciers thaw
    and find there's nothing perma
about frost

let there be the shock
of release

    from petrified attitude
into melted light
and fuzzy velocity,

liberation
from angle
    and the deep blue plaque
of fear

into pure continuum.

A kind of joy even.

Here then is the prayer
(and the time is always three a.m.):

let liquefaction
not mean
liquidation.

'Dying is hard work'

The hospice worker told Jules,
and I think of her now
in a Newcastle hotel room,

looking out at the gizzard
and viscera of a construction site,
its engorged innards,
        empurpled
with intent,

here where labour room is hospice
and workshop abattoir,

here in this laboratory livid
with desire

where aliveness
is unguarded butchery,

and the lust of mortar
for definition

is as old, as shameless, as the need
of pediment and girder

for swamp
        and amnesia,

reminding us,
reminding us all the time

that birthing is a hard business.

    Dying too.

Goddess

(after Neeli Mariamman)

> It's enough
> to sit alone
> and gaze at you
> three-eyed Goddess.
> Who needs to go meditate?
>
> ABHIRAMI BHATTAR
(translated from the Tamil)

Those who go to the great temples
of Perur and Avinashi
know nothing of her.

She's isn't interested
in being the flavour
of a few thousand years.

She's been around
since the planet was a seizure

of waterness
and protoplasm.

In the great garrulity of gods
she is silent.

She'll never be the life
of the party

but she's not concerned with the party.

She is life –
twisty blue nerve fire –

life local,
life perennial,

the goddess Neeli Mariamman.

On Tuesday afternoons
in the month of May

she erupts
into an epilepsy of form,

ballooning a small nut-brown priest
into prescience,

and as he foams and curdles
his eyes sightless,

she prescribes remedies
to a peasant plagued
by blisters in his gum,

advises the crone to be patient
with her daughter-in-law

for women must be wooed
and fear must not spawn a new generation.

Then she turns towards you
and her eyes are craters,

her light molten jaggery
and burnt almond,

her tongue is toxic shock,
her gaze tundra.

She is the shockingly naked wire
at the centre of the world

where your future is a long burnt-out
morning star.

The universe is her hamlet,
she says,

a flystain
in her monarchy.

Her laughter is her empire.

Goddess II

(after Linga Bhairavi)

In her burning rainforest
silence is so alive
you can hear

listening.

Goddess III

(after Linga Bhairavi)

She sucks you
into the raging blue wilderness
of her womb

where you wear her
like cocoon,
you wear her
like story,
you wear her
like cosmos

through which you reel,

    crazily
unborn.

Memo I

Reaching for the summit,
    but never forgetting coast –

the melancholy
    of harbours by dusk,

women in summer dresses
    on the streets of Nice,

the festive blaze
    of vendors on Juhu beach,

evenings alive
    with hope and buttered corn.

Never forgetting,
    never forgetting even for a minute,

mean sea level.

Memo II

To choose
    the right table,

the right quarrel,
    the right gaze.

Not the conference
    of hungry eyes,

but the fellowship
    of those who stand aslant,

multilingual,
    listening,

their shadows
    four-footed, their wisdom

angostura, their hearts
    green sun and groundwater.

Those who hope to cut through the fog,
    uncurdle the dream,

but still weep
    unoriginally

for the moon.

In Praise of Conversations

Those that might happen one day
    in Tbilisi,
        in Yangon,

            in Aizawl,
                  Positano.

Those that rose
like yeast and melted
like butter in Irani restaurants in Bombay.

That which happens in silence
with the poet whose whisky
turns gold when the ships hoot
at midnight on the Ganga,

the one that lingers
    aromatic,
        incomplete,
in a tavern by the river
where the light is pure Chianti,

the one still replayed
over Nagarjuna
    or Spinoza
in university cafeterias.

The one on a beach in Accra
where the moon
was crushed opal underfoot.

The one I never figured
about the politics
of saying an Indian paddy field

was as green
as a Scottish meadow.
                    (And so?)

Those that waft across the ages
through Persian gardens
and the foetid bylanes
of Cairo fish markets.

Those that stormed and raged
but now simply shiver
        like the slurry
                of floating islands
                        on Lake Inle,
like the one that paused
for a very long time
when I flung books
out of an office window
(that we now laughingly deem
apocryphal).

The ones that meander
into truths,

the ones that lie
in parentheses,

the ones that lie,

the ones that never began
(because you never listened
and then because you couldn't hear
and because I was too afraid to speak),

the one at a grey stone table
with the friend I've always known –
in a place I thought I recognised later as Tibet –

and the great roar of happiness
so difficult to forget.

It happened years,
years before we met,

and the world when I woke
was wet, alive and keeling,
keeling right over with laughter –

Afterword

And as long
as there are wizened men
sipping ochre tea

in a shop with the aluminium roof
down the road

and the clerk
with the absurdly radiant smile

in the post-office behind
the municipal school
near the Mariamman temple,

it may not be so difficult,
Avvaiyar thinks,
even if friends seem far away
or distracted

to decant quietly
into some dawn,

leaving behind
a smudge,

then perhaps nothing at all.

Some days she suspects
the plot is thicker,
the weave richer,
the fibre finer,
the story more outrageous,
the longing more contagious
than she once supposed.

Some days she suspects
all tales unravel,
all fibres fray,
all threads unspool

       into an exuberance
of yarn.

Some days she suspects
she might even ride
a Persian carpet to the stars.

ACKNOWLEDGEMENTS

Acknowledgements are due to the editors of the following publications in which some of these poems, at times in different versions, first appeared: *Afur* 3 and 4, *The Hindu*, *The Indian Express*, *Plume* (Issue 76), *Journal of the Poetry Society* (India), *Muse India*, *IQ-Indian Quarterly*, *Indian Literature*, *Project Boast* (Triarchy Press), *Drunken Boat* (24), and *All the Worlds Between* (Yoda Press).